Putting Social Media To Work 2.0:
For Your Small Business

Gemma Dale
@HR_Gem

Tim Scott
@TimScottHR

Cover art by **Simon Heath**
@SimonHeath1

> Throughout this book we have given Twitter handles (read on if you're not sure what that means!) wherever possible for named individuals or organisations. These are shown as @username.

First edition: December 2016

Copyright © Gemma Dale & Tim Scott

All rights reserved. Permission granted to reproduce for personal and educational use only. Commercial copying, hiring, lending is prohibited.

From 251112 to here - so far.

Contents

Why you should care about social media 5
What the heck is social media anyway? 7
Facts and Figures 8
Rule Number One 10
Even more about different types of social stuff 11
What has social ever done for us? 16
What is in it for you? 19
Rule Number Two 22
Social Selling 23
Rule Number Three. 27
Getting Started 28
Rule Number Four 30
More practical stuff 31
Adoption of Social 32
Rule Number Five 34
Return on Investment 35
Rule Number Six 39
#Facepalm – how to avoid getting it wrong 40
Giving it a Go 43
Myth Busting 45
Rule Number Seven 48
Picking Your Platforms 51
Blogs 60
Finding stuff to share 63

Rule Number Eight 65

The Marketing Mix 66

A Very Important P 67

Social Media That Rocks 69

Rule Number Nine 73

Final Thoughts (Almost) 74

Tools and Techniques 76

A Social Media and Technology Glossary 78

And Finally: Get Started on Twitter & LinkedIn 88

Why you should care about social media

Seth Godin described social media as the greatest shift of our generation. We tend to agree with him. We have also heard it described as the greatest shift in the workplace since the industrial revolution. We believe that it arguably offers greater opportunities to rethink some of the old ways of working than organisations and individual professionals have had before.

Social media has become a ubiquitous subject. Discussions abound on how to recruit with social media, how to get your CEO to be social, how to sell socially, headlines about employees who have posted something dubious finding themselves on the receiving end of their P45, even people who are divorcing because of Facebook behaviour. But for every individual and organisation embracing it, there is another who is fearful of it and another that just hasn't got a clue what all the fuss is about.

The world has changed, is changing, is going to change some more. It has always been the case. And right at the centre of this intensifying change is technology and social technology in particular. Driving new ways of working, communicating and creating new opportunities; for organisations and individuals alike. The old rules no longer apply. We must rethink the way we work, sell, engage, communicate, talk to customers and build and manage our reputations and brands.

We live in an increasingly open and transparent world. Many of us think nothing now of putting our entire CV online for people to view. Even if you don't, you probably have a **LinkedIn** page with the same information on. We tweet our everyday lives and share our thoughts with the world. Or our followers at least. There is no home time/work time dividing line any more, just increasingly blurred lines. For good or for bad, we are constantly connected. Always on. Anywhere and any when. In the office or the **Coffice**.

For businesses and their owners, there is an important simple truth of the new social world. Your customers are there. Your employees are there. Your competitors are too. People are talking about your brand online, whether you like it or not. There is a saying in the social media world; the conversation is happening anyway so you might as well be part of it. Resisting this truth is akin to denying the existence of the telephone.

Social has the power to change everything; it is that impactful. How we communicate and collaborate at a fundamental level. How we sell and market our services. How we lead and how we learn. How we engage and communicate with the people that work for us and the people that buy from us. How we actually do the day job. Who has the power? Who is considered to be a leader? Where we physically sit to do the work that we do. No longer are we limited to or by our immediate team, organisation, locality, time zone.

So in this little book, we are going to aim to do a few things. Firstly, explain why understanding social and getting social is so important for individuals and organisations alike, and why, whatever your personal view on all things social media, you cannot ignore it. We are going to share own experiences about what social has done for us and other stories from those who have successfully used social media to build their businesses. And then we will give you some ideas about how you can get started, and some key rules to follow.

When it comes to social media, there is stuff that you can pay for and the free stuff. For the purposes of this book, we are assuming that a small business doesn't have a big marketing budget, so we are going to focus on what you do yourself, without a big financial investment.

We recognise that people will come to this book with varying levels of knowledge about social media and technology – from ninja to newbie.

> As you go through the book, you'll come across some more technical words and/or jargon terms that are highlighted in **bold**. This means they are explained in a bit more detail in the Glossary at the back.

Are you sitting comfortably? Because we're about to enter the social world.

What the heck is social media anyway?

When a lot of people hear the term social media, their first thought is of networks like Facebook or Twitter. They think about the social networking side of social media. But at its broadest, social media is much, much more than that.

At its most basic level, social media is about any platform or application that allows you to share content with other people, sometimes publicly and sometimes to a prescribed audience chosen by you, and that allow you to participate in networking activity. It takes many forms.

It does include those social applications we have already mentioned.

It also includes **blogs** and **vlogs** like Tumblr and WordPress.

It includes content communities like **YouTube**.

It includes professional networking like **LinkedIn**.

It includes messaging and photo apps like **Snapchat**.

It includes community sites like **Slack** and Google+.

It includes forums and virtual gaming.

It includes social bookmarking.

It includes collaborative (often called "**crowdsourced**") projects like Wikipedia.

Social media is online technology that enables the sharing of ideas and information and allows comment and discussion and debate, whether on a tablet or a PC or a mobile.

There are two very important facts that you need to know about social media. Firstly, it is a world that is constantly evolving. Any list of social media applications and platforms will be out of date the moment it was written. And secondly, its use is increasing exponentially, including across all generations.

Facts and Figures

Figures sourced from the United Nations show that the number of people using the internet has now reached 3.4 billion. We are approaching the point where 50% of the planet's population are using the internet. Yes, you did read that correctly.

At the same time, traditional methods of communication like email, **snail mail** and the phone have declined. Fewer people have a home landline. Some organisations are going entirely email free. Others are only accepting job applications via Twitter.

These numbers get out of date as soon as they are printed, but at the time of writing in late 2016, 73% of UK adults use the internet daily, and 50% of them are using social networking sites. Internet users have an average of over five social media accounts. Every second, there are 12 new social media users added.

Facebook has 1.7 billion users, 23% of whom access the site more than five times a day. Facebook and WhatsApp handle between them 60 million messages every single day.

LinkedIn now has 300 million members. **Pinterest** has 100 million members. 500 million tweets are sent every day by over 320 million users. 1 1 million micro blogs on **Tumblr**. 110 million more post their photos over at **Instagram**. And **YouTube** has over 1 billion users worldwide.

Four out of five purchases are influenced by online content. Over 80% of businesses saying that they research and find suppliers online.

By 2025, 5 billion people will be connected by mobile devices.

Part of this extraordinary growth in internet use is based on the smart phone, something 53% of us now carry around in our pockets. A tipping point has been reached and breached with now more than half of internet connections made via a mobile device. With the exception of **LinkedIn** - which remains mostly desktop - all of the main social media sites are accessed primarily via a mobile device.

When it comes to using social media, surveys vary. But what we do know for certain is that it is not just something for younger people.

Profiles of sites vary too of course: Snapchat attracts a much younger user base, whereas over on Twitter their fastest growing demographic is the 55-64 age bracket.

Remember the days when you had to sit at your computer and use a dial-up modem, with its characteristic screeching bleeping sound to access the internet? Broadband used to be a nice to have, luxury item. Now it is a life essential to most. **Cognitive Assistants** are on the way. **Wearable** technology is going mainstream. Low cost **cloud computing** has become widely available. Phones are no longer just phones, they are **converged devices**.

As is commonly quoted, there is more computer power in your washing machine than it took to send a man to the moon. By 2020 it is estimated that computers will have the power of the human brain. If it isn't already, pretty soon your washing machine will be connected to the internet too as part of what is being called the "**Internet of things**" – in other words, the internet will become integral to many day to day activities that currently don't involve computers at all.

We are all social now. This isn't about one particular platform or social network. It is about completely new ways of working, selling, communicating. A potential promise of something better, perhaps.

Rule Number One

Social is only one part of the marketing mix.

Social does not replace more traditional forms of marketing, like email, newsletters, or some good old face to face networking. It is simply another way to reach your target customers, but with some added benefits.

Marketing has always been about having a mix. Social media should be just one part of that mix. If you do it well, you can integrate it with those more traditional forms and make all of it work together, in the most effective way possible.

There's more about that to come later on.

Even more about different types of social stuff

We have written this chapter especially for social media newbies. It's an overview of the main platforms and types of all things social.

The most important thing to note is that this chapter will be out of date almost as soon as we have written it. There is new stuff coming along all the time; we've only mentioned the main ones or this chapter would be longer than the rest of the book combined. You can't do them all, so don't even try.

Twitter

Our favourite platform. We actually met on Twitter, and organised most of this book through its private messaging function, the handy 'DM' (which stands for direct message). The second biggest social media platform out there.

Twitter is built about one simple premise: you can only post messages made up of fewer than 140 characters. You'd probably be surprised by what you can achieve within that limit: it's entirely possible to share images, videos, links and just straightforward comments. Out of all the platforms, you will find more of a blurring of the professional and the personal here. Twitter is great for people and great for brands.

Blogging

We are both bloggers and we are passionate advocates of it. Blogging is basically self-publishing. No longer is **content** the preserve of journalists or paid academics. With 60 million **WordPress** blogs, people are out there, putting their thoughts and ideas into the world for others to see. Blogging is a disruptive technology, in a good way.

Blogs are a rich stream of learning. They offer ideas straight to your computer screen, tablet or pocket. Reading them is a great way to engage with some brilliant thinking - all for free. The other power of blogs is their interactivity. People leave comments and engage with the blogger and his or her content. Blogs are generally more reflective pieces than the short snappy stuff you get on Twitter. They are also a bit more personal than the more formal business articles found on somewhere like **LinkedIn**.

There are people blogging on pretty much everything. From leadership to fitness, from fashion to music. People blog about their mental health, their politics, their favourite recipes. Work, personal, and everything in between. We'd love you to read our blogs. We think they are brilliant. But if thoughts about the worlds of work and Human Resources are not your cup of tea, then you will surely find something that works for you.

Whilst we love blogging, it is undoubtedly one of the more time-consuming of social activities in terms of content creation and maintenance. We think it is worth it though! Later on, we will talk a little more about why you might want to blog for the benefits of your business.

LinkedIn

The professional networking site. Think of it like your online CV, your career or business elevator pitch. It is supposed to be a professional networking site, although some people still seem to get it confused with Facebook - and increasingly so, we have observed. For us, it is one of those sites that you kind of *need* to be on, rather than anything you can get really passionate about. We don't like the user experience all that much. More and more of what used to be free on the site you now have to pay for. If it wasn't so ubiquitous, we would probably suggest going somewhere less boring instead.

These niggles aside, it does have its positives too. Having a strong profile is undoubtedly good for your personal brand as it allows you to showcase your achievements, look for work and be found by people who are recruiting. But for chat, for groups, for building relationships, we prefer other places. However, as we will say repeatedly, it is about picking what is right for you and your business, so don't let us put you off with our personal preferences.

Google+ (or G+)

Possibly a little underrated. Very good for **Search Engine Optimisation**, which means if you want your stuff to appear high up on a Google search it is good to have your content there. If you are local business it's important to have a G+ account, as it allows you to put a pin in Google maps showing your location. You also need a G+

account to create a YouTube channel. Once you have an account you can also do Google Hangouts – like Skype but better.

Pinterest

Think of it like an online notice board: a place for pinning images, videos and links onto your own noticeboards, which can be public or private. You will find everything on there from recipes, wedding ideas, fitness inspiration and motivational quotes. It's definitely growing as a platform, and can have a corporate angle too, especially if your product or service is quite photogenic.

Instagram

It's all about sharing pictures and video. You can follow and be followed, and can have an open account or keep it private. You can comment on other people's stuff too, as well as stalk - sorry, we mean *follow* - celebrities. You can link it up across all of your other social media accounts so that your photos are uploaded to them all. It is at least partially responsible for the rise of the selfie. The best bit about it of all is that you can apply filters and all sorts of effects to your pictures, making sure that you (or your product) look as good as you can before you unleash your latest photographic masterpiece on an unsuspecting world.

Facebook

The one everyone knows about. Used to be cool, now perhaps less so. It has been slightly abandoned by younger folks as their parents and grandparents get on there. We won't say much more about Facebook, because we reckon if you don't know what it is you must have been sleeping under a rock. Just one thing to note – as well as the personal profile (remember to check your privacy settings please for those concerned with their personal brand!) you can do business on here too. If you are a local business, or in the business to consumer market then you might want to think about a business page. But under no circumstances should you mix the two.

Also just released into the wild is what was being known as Facebook at Work, but has been re-christened "Workplace" (although it's the same thing) - an internal social network for colleagues within a corporate network that looks and feels like Facebook.

Periscope

An app that is owned by Twitter and allows you to live stream video over the internet. It includes an option to make videos entirely public or just available to selected viewers. Because of the link with Twitter it also allows users to tweet a link to their video content. It is particularly useful for sharing content from events and conferences. It remains to be seen how it will be affected by Facebook's alternative, Facebook Live.

Snapchat

This one is a messaging app. Users can take pictures or videos and add text or drawings to them, then share them with their friends. The user decides how long the 'snaps' are available for – but it's usually just a few seconds, which limits its business application a little – but there are still brands out there making the most of it. It has quite a young user demographic – the **selfie** is a very popular on SnapChat. Accounts can be public or private. It's still a niche site for now.

WhatsApp

Essentially a messaging tool – globally the most popular in 2015 with 600 million active users. It is now owned by Facebook – which has got some people worried about privacy and what Facebook will do with all of that information... You can send messages between individuals and groups of people, including pictures and links. It also allows sharing of pictures and links. It used to require a small annual subscription fee but this has now been removed – and as a result it is becoming very widely used in both business and personal applications.

YouTube

Some people don't really think of YouTube as a social network. But it is about sharing content (of the video variety) and allowing people to comment on it. Thousands and thousands of hours of video footage are uploaded to YouTube every day. It is now one of the biggest search engines in the world. You will find a whole range of stuff here - TV clips, **Vlogs**, "how to" videos created by people in their garages, corporate content, music videos. If it can be filmed it will be on there. And we will leave the rest of that to your imagination.

Slack

A cross between a social media platform and an old-style internet message board. It's basically a project management-type app that is allegedly used by NASA. It allows you to get a team together in one digital place, run different conversation threads, share documents and the like. It encourages quick and easy internal collaboration.

There are many more social media platforms than just these few described here; we have simply picked a few of the biggest ones. Some are more about producing and sharing content, some more about chatting. Any book that tried to cover them all would be out of date very quickly – probably before it was printed. You can never be on every platform, there are simply too many. Our advice is just take a look, play around, and find one or two platforms that work for you and your business, and in particular where your customers are likely to be.

In a later chapter we will explore a bit more about which ones might work for you and share some top tips for getting started on the platform.

What has social ever done for us?

We wanted to take the opportunity to share our personal stories. To show what social media has done for us, our careers and our learning. The opportunities it has given to us, and can perhaps give to you too.

Firstly, we met on social media. Twitter to be precise. And then we met in real life, and this book, and a friendship, was born.

Gem's story

I sent my first tweet as @HR_Gem on 1 June 2011. Like many Twitter users I started off doing quite a bit of watching and looking. Or lurking, to give it its proper terminology. Just letting the content come to me and following HR people. When people join social networks there tends to be a bit of an evolution. Watching to begin with, followed by building up the confidence to go a little further; doing a little sharing and chatting. As people start to follow you back, you start to be more comfortable in beginning dialogue, and slowly move to a more active phase.

I started to chat regularly to people within the HR community. One day in February 2013, I tweeted about how nice it would be to meet some **tweeps** in the flesh, or as they say on Twitter, IRL (in real life). I found out about a networking event for people in HR and the like, organised via social media channels, called Connecting HR Manchester.

So I booked a hotel for the night and off I went. I suppose it was a bit like going on a blind date, only with 25 people. As the evening wore on, more and more rather awesome and interesting people turned up. It was HR, and it was social, and it was engaging.

Of course, a drink was taken. Then we went to a chip shop, where four of us preceded to have a very heated debate about the future of employee voice post trade union decline. Then there was some arm wrestling. It was that sort of evening. But aside from the jokes, I made some excellent contacts that have turned into friendships, collaborations and all sorts of opportunities, including this very book.

Eventually I went on and started my blog, "People Stuff". I've gone on to blog from events, speak at conferences and at universities, and write for the HR Director magazine. I've collaborated on eBooks, all though my social media connections. None of these opportunities would have happened but for social media. I have also been a state of almost continuous learning, beginning every morning when I check my timeline over the first coffee of the day. I have an amazing network and am part of a community, all in the device in my pocket.

Tim's story

I sent my first tweet as @TimScottHR on 1 November 2012. I was encouraged to tweet by a former colleague who told me he found it very useful professionally and thought I would too. For most of my career I'd operated as the "standalone" HR person in my organisation, which meant that apart from reading the odd magazine and attending the occasional employment law update, I didn't "network" with other HR people that much, so it seemed a good way to get involved with other people in my professional area and build up some contacts.

At this stage I have to confess that I'd actually had a different Twitter account since 2009. I did what seems to be mandatory for most people on joining Twitter in that I followed a few celebrities and a handful of people I knew. I didn't really "get" it to be honest and as a result I hardly ever checked it. It was only when I discovered the community of HR people that actively use it that it started to make sense. I think of it like learning a language – it takes a while to get your head around the general approach but once you've got a basic idea, the only way to develop is simply to dive in and get speaking it. You might make the odd grammatical mistake but native speakers will get what you mean and overlook the occasional mishap.

It isn't overstating it to say that after joined Twitter, my career was completely reinvigorated. Rather like Gem's story, sending that first tweet started a stone rolling that has seen me speaking at conferences, making videos for the CIPD, joining international project teams to improve the world of work, writing for HR publications and occasionally appearing in print media! Oh and writing the odd book too. There are people I'm now proud to number amongst my closest friends who I would never have met without social media. I've also transformed how I approach my work – I'm convinced I got my last role largely on the strength of the knowledge and self-confidence (and the odd direct quote) I'd got from my social network. None of these things would have happened if I'd have carried on being that unintentionally insular HR person, closed away in my thinking and practice.

Although I'm yet to have a chip shop arm wrestle. There's still time...

Later, we will feature some professionals who have managed to develop their business through the use of social media. Stay tuned!

What is in it for you?

We've talked about what social has done for us professionally. But what can it do for you and your business?

Anyone who runs their own business already has significant demands on their time and energy. So this social media stuff might just seem like one more chore on the never ending to-do list.

But failing to engage with social media might mean that you are missing out on very real opportunities. Opportunities to engage with current or potential customers, an opportunity to build your personal brand and put yourself out there as an expert, or maybe find other people or businesses to collaborate with.

We won't like to you: engaging socially does take some time and effort. But the benefits, both personally and organisationally, can be significant.

For us, it comes down to five broad areas.

- Connecting
- Learning
- Sharing
- Personal brand
- Listening

Connecting

Let's face it: networking is something that we know we are supposed to do, but doesn't come easy to many of us – the face to face type of networking certainly. All that walking into a room and introducing yourself to people you don't know stuff. Social media is basically about connecting people. Social media makes this much easier. It is about building your network, and in particular, finding new and potential customers. With social, geography does not get in the way. You can network with other professionals in your industry – and indeed your target customer groups - across the globe if you want to. Often, connections that are made on line can turn into face to face meetings and connections in the future. That is exactly how we met!

Learning

Social media is a constant stream of ideas; new things, blogs, podcasts, tweets, video. Straight to the device in your pocket. There for you to consume when it suits you. No longer do you have to go on a training course, sit from nine until five and dutifully watch all of the PowerPoint slides. And if you follow and connect with the right people you don't even have to go looking for it, it will come to you. We love blogs for learning. 500 or so words, easy to consume, something for everyone. The truth is, whatever business you run, whatever professional you are in, you need to keep up to date and relevant to your market and your customers. Social just makes this easy to do. And then you can share that learning with your customers and connections. Often, especially for the self-employed individual or small business, there isn't lots of money or time available for formal courses and the like. But there is plenty of learning available in the social world. It is all out there, and a whole heck of a lot of it is free.

Sharing

Social media has made things much more open, more transparent than in the past. People now do a presentation and put it on **Slideshare** for other people to see. You have an idea and get it out there on a blog. Sharing your own stuff, finding good stuff from other people, and just putting it out there. Social media is reciprocal. You share other people's stuff and they will share yours – including information about your products and services.

Personal Brand

If you want to develop your personal brand then social media is a pretty awesome way to doing it. We know plenty of self-employed professionals who build their business around social media. Their blogs, Twitter feeds and LinkedIn profiles are a showcase for their work, as well as pretty much all of their advertising and networking activity too. Social gives you the opportunity to differentiate yourself from everyone else, put yourself out there as a bit of a "thought leader", to coin an overused phrase. It makes you a real person. It is an old saying that people buy from people. But there is often truth to be found in clichés. Having a face to your brand can be a big influencer in purchasing decisions. It is much more personal than a company website can ever be.

Listening

Want to know what your customers or target customers are talking about? What they are thinking and feeling? And most importantly – what they are saying about *your* business? Whether you believe it or not, they are doing those things in the social space. Social gives you an opportunity to meet with them where they are. More about that when we get to rule number eight.

Of course with every opportunity also comes some risk. More on that later, too.

Rule Number Two

> **Social is a long game.**

You won't pick up a new customer with your first tweet. What social media does allow you to do however, is build a long term relationship and increase your brand's reach and presence.

We said earlier that social is about connecting. In our day jobs, we both have responsibility for selecting suppliers. Both of us regularly use providers on everything from training to communications to IT software, from organisations that we have engaged with first in the social space.

Social will help you find customers or potential customers. But we'd like to suggest that this isn't the way to approach it. If instead, you approach social media with the aim to be engaging, make connections, share useful information (both yours and other peoples) and build relationships, then the business and the customers will follow.

Let it grow. It will take time. Keep putting content out there. Keeping engaging, internally and externally. It will build momentum, slowly but surely.

Social Selling

Social media has changed the sales and marketing landscape, and disrupted the traditional sales cycle. We still believe we have only seen a small part of the potential. More is still to come.

People buy online of course. But even if they don't always complete the transaction there, our purchasing decisions are hugely influenced in the online space all the same. We check out **crowdsourced** product reviews (think Trip Advisor); we listen to what our friends say online. This includes social media too.

In the old days, marketing had the consumer in very much a passive, receiving sort of space. Whether it was a TV advert broadcasting at you while you sat on the sofa, a mass-mailed press release, a billboard at the side of the road or junk mail through the letter box, they sent and you received. The brand told you that they were awesome. You might buy or you might not. If you bought and you liked it, you might buy some more and you might tell a few of your friends.

Consumer behaviour has changed. We are much more active than we used to be, in terms of our purchasing behaviour, our interactivity with brands and our public willingness to share our consumer experiences – the good and the bad. Social media means that there is interaction taking place between the buyer and the seller. It has also increased the power of that consumer, who can take that action anywhere and any when. Now, you want other people to tell other people you are awesome. Let's face it, who are you more likely to believe – the corporate message, or your friend that just used the product?

Social media is influencing our buying decisions like never before. It is also changing our consumer behaviour in other ways. We learn about products, brands and services through our social feeds. We complain about poor service, including the offending company in the tweet. We are exposed to celebrities waxing lyrical about their favourite brands. We have more information at our finger tips than we ever have had.

So, like with all things social, there is an opportunity and there is a risk.

The opportunity is to engage with your customers and potential customers in a totally new way. More interactive, more dialogue, more about building a long term relationship. A way to build your brand, showcase your products and services, tell your stories. Social media can give your brand a personality; make it come to life beyond the corporate, often formal messaging. Social becomes the face of your brand and your story, just like the shop assistant in the high street store or the receptionist at corporate HQ.

The risks are many too. Employees can damage your brand (or, as we like to say in HR, bring the company into disrepute) by inappropriate sharing or commenting. It is just as easy for your social media team to make a mistake too. Take the example of a clothing brand American Apparel. Their (young) social media manager tweeted a picture of the exploding space shuttle Challenger on the 4th July. He'd just been looking for an image. An image that was immediately recognisable as something terrible, to people of a certain age. Lesson: don't hand your social media account over to inexperienced people just because they are young and therefore must understand it. This is just not true.

In 2008, a United Airlines passenger saw baggage handlers throwing his guitar onto a plane. When he retrieved it, the guitar was damaged. He asked the airline to pay for the damage caused, but they refused. So the passenger wrote a song about it, and posted the video on You Tube. To date, it has had over 14 million views. That same passenger then wrote a book about the experience and is now a conference speaker. So social media can seriously damage you too; if you give crappy customer service, you might just go viral.

A good understanding of social media is now a core competency for any sales and marketing professional. The benefits are simple:

- Social media allows consumers to build trust with a brand and to build long term relationships with consumers.

- Social media goes to where the consumers are, in the place that they are interacting every day. It allows you to engage with those groups and just maybe make them your fans or advocates.

- Social makes your brand visible and enhances brand awareness.

- Social media is real time not slow time.

- Social allows you to position yourself and your business as an authority. Maybe even a thought leader.

- For the smaller company or the self-employed professional, social can get you a great web presence even if you haven't got a huge budget for marketing or a fancy website.

- Social media, especially blogging, is great for improving your **search engine optimisation**.

- You can easily monitor your competitor activity, as well as listen to what people are saying about you and your brand in the social space.

Here's a simple tale we were told by a former colleague (so we think it's true!). He was in a (national chain) coffee shop waiting to meet a friend who only drank tea. He discovered that the shop he was in had run out of tea and tweeted his friend who was running a bit late that they had no tea. Quick as a flash, a rival, smaller coffee shop just a few doors down the street tweeted them both that they had plenty of tea as well as fine coffee. The end result was that they moved their meeting to the rival coffee shop and the national chain lost the business – all because of active, real time social media marketing.

Having said that, the dangers are simple too:

- Doing social badly is worse than not doing it at all. This includes not being sufficiently present, either in terms of content provision, but also in terms of responding to questions or comments.

- You need to be fast to respond to your customers, especially to anything negative.

- It needs to be maintained – from a business perspective, content, as they say, is king. You need to continually put good, relevant content out there for people to see. Once a month won't cut it.

- Poor content can damage your brand.

- If you offer poor customer service, poor value for money and the like – this will surface on social. But it will do that whether you are there or not.

There is one important point that can be a risk if you get it wrong at the outset. When it comes to marketing, social media is one part of the marketing mix and the overall strategy. It is an "as well as" and not instead of. If you treat it as an entirely separate thing, you will never fully exploit its potential.

At the risk of repeating ourselves: in social media there is both new opportunity and new risk. One of the people we admire in this space is Gary Vaynerchuck (find him on Twitter as @garyvee), and he has a great message that we think is relevant here. He says that you need to market your business in the year that you are living in. And frankly, that means socially.

Rule Number Three.

Be sensible.

You can think what you like. You can say what you like. You can pretty much say what you like on social media too, unless you are breaking the law. But a little common sense would tell you that publicly broadcasting whatever comes to mind, especially when it includes expletives, obscenities and insults, pictures of you under the influence or anything containing discrimination, nudity or the like is going to cause you an issue if that particular account is linked in any way to your job. What can make your personal brand can break it too. This sounds obvious but plenty of people get it wrong all the same. History is replete with people who have posted a social media status in haste and repented at leisure.

Common sense. Something that should be exercised alongside your social media use at all times. People have varying standards on social media, as they do in all aspects of life. We quite like the approach of one of our mutual tweeps (Twitter slang for "friends on Twitter" – from Tweeple, ie Twitter people) which is to ask himself before tweeting:

- Would it offend my Mum?

- What would my boss think?

In terms of rules, we reckon that's about all you need to follow.

Oh - and never, ever tweet whilst drunk.

Getting Started

We have talked about the what and the why of social media. Hopefully you're feeling encouraged to have a go if you don't already, so now it is time to talk about the how - what you need to think about when getting social yourself or where you work. We are going to start with some of our top tips, and then dig a little deeper into a few.

First things first

Whether you are looking at social as an individual or in a business context, any social media strategy has to start with one question: why.

There are plenty of people having a go at social media. Some of them are doing it because they think they should or because everyone else is doing it. But without a clearly defined 'why' then it will be difficult to get the most from it and focus efforts. Neither will it be easy to measure results and adapt your approach accordingly.

If it is on the personal side, maybe it is about improving (or establishing) your personal brand, or maybe you are initially just looking to get social for fun. For a business it could be about developing the company brand, supporting other sales and marketing efforts, or simply finding new customers. Whatever it is, you need to come up with some aims and desired outcomes. Everything else flows from there. Without a why, it's a bit like just jumping on a bandwagon, and your efforts won't be sufficiently focused or your outcomes capable of review.

So first of all, decide why you are doing it at all. This doesn't need to be huge. Some small goals at first are just fine.

Our other warning, especially if you are thinking about what social means for you and our business, is that you will need to make an investment in social, whether in time, resources or money. There is nothing worse than looking up a company and finding an abandoned profile, or sending a tweet to them and hearing nothing back.

Just because most social media is free to sign up, there is sometimes the misconception that it is cheap, and it is easy. Well this ain't necessarily so. Doing social well takes time and effort, and measuring the return on investment isn't all that straightforward either.

So set your goals, and keep them under review. And then set some more when you have reached them.

Rule Number Four

You can't do it all.

You will need to pick your platforms. Better to do a couple really, really well and build up a following than try and do ten platforms averagely. Our thoughts on that are coming up soon.

More practical stuff

If you run a small business there is some practical stuff to think about, especially if you employ other people. Policies, employment law, and training – these things are slightly dull but important.

So if you employ people, here are a couple of thoughts from us.

If the people in your business don't understand social media, then you will have to take a little time to make the case for it (or buy them a copy of this book). Explain clearly to people what is in it for them – and your business – to get social. Find and explain the benefits: brand awareness, increased sales, an opportunity to talk to your customers and so on. And as well as explaining the benefits, explain the risks of not being there too (namely, your competitors will be!).

Training is key. Once people understand the why, help them with the how. Social can feel scary when you first use it. Although to some people it is part of their everyday, there are others to whom it is completely new. People worry about what to tweet, what they can and can't share. Social is full of new terminology and involves technology that is unfamiliar to some. So make it easy for folks to get on board and join in. The glossary at the back of this book will help!

Get a policy. It doesn't have to be long. It doesn't have to ban a load of stuff. But you do need to tell people what you consider is okay and what is not, out there in that social space. Be very clear about what might be the outcome if there is inappropriate behaviour in the social space.

Share success and reward involvement. Social needs to be reinforced, especially in its early days when it is new and different. When people see it working this will help it become part of the everyday. So if you get a lead through social and in turns into real live business, then make sure you show and tell.

Be the role model – especially if you are the business leader. Leaders getting in there and getting sharing can send the message that this is an okay way to spend your time at work.

Adoption of Social

When it comes to all things new you may be already familiar with Roger's Innovation Adoption Curve (Google it if not!).

This measures the extent to which innovations flow through society. Most things, especially technology, tend to follow a similar pattern both in society and within organisations. Early on is the innovator and the early adopter; those folks who are ahead of the curve and want the new stuff first. They are the ones queuing up all night outside a store getting the latest gadget so they have their hands on it as soon as the doors open. Everyone else slowly catches up at a varying pace, eventually landing with the late majority and then the laggards who catch up last of all.

How to spot a laggard:

- They see no reason to upgrade their Nokia 3210

- When you ask them if they saw your instant message, they ask you what one of those is

- They have used a fax machine (probably in the last week)

- They make comments like 'isn't Twitter all about telling people what you had for breakfast?'

We jest. A little. Generally, we are probably in the middle of this journey when it comes to social media. It has been around for some time. For many people and organisations, it has been part of their everyday life for some time. For others, it is still a world of strange language and something for "the kids".

There are a couple of things that usually impact upon how well technology is adopted both within an organisation and personally too. There is something called the Technology Adoption Model. Not everyone likes it, and it has been criticised as being too simplistic. But we think it works for the social world. The first thing that impacts adoption (or otherwise) of social media is the extent to which people see the benefit to themselves – what problem is it solving? The official model calls it 'perceived usefulness'. We tend to think of it as the 'What's in it for me' (WIIFM) question.

And the WIIFM will vary from person to person.

What all of this means is that your customers or target customers will be adopting social media in a similar way. Some will be using it excessively and have fully incorporated it into their lives. Like us, they will spend quite a bit of time looking at their phones. For others, they aren't there all that much at all. This is why you still need to maintain a mix of all marketing approaches. As much as we are advocates of all things social, it can never be the full solution.

Rule Number Five

> **Think carefully about personal versus private.**

If you are using social media for your business, then you might want to think about separating it entirely from any personal accounts. We've seen people who use their business Facebook account as their personal one too. But do you really want people who look you up as they are interested in working for or with you, finding some pictures of you out with your mates, or perhaps photos of your children? It doesn't look very professional, and for most businesses it doesn't set the right tone.

When you are deliberately keeping accounts private as they are nothing to do with your business or brand, then consider carefully your privacy settings. If someone goes a Google search of your name or company name, you want them to find your professional activities and shares, and not some drunken photos on your personal Facebook page.

And if you have never Google searched yourself, this might be the moment to try, and see what comes up. Disclaimer: we take absolutely no responsibility for what happens next.

Return on Investment

Ah yes, the elusive ROI. Proof that your efforts are working and delivering a desired outcome.

Let us start by saying this is a tricky one. It is hard to put a value on a relationship and a connection. When it comes to social you are measuring something slightly different than you are with other forms of sales and marketing: influence and visibility. Some of the connections you will make on social will lead to something, some will not, and some will lead to something far down the road. But when considering implementing social from a brand or marketing point of view, much of the same can be said about the more traditional methods too.

When a social media friend of ours gets asked the question, as he often does, he tends to go on the offensive with a question right back. 'What is the value of your mum?' It makes a certain point. Namely, that there are some things that are hard to quantify – but have an unquestionable value.

There is something of a leap of faith about being a social business. But that isn't enough for some people. Especially those finance types. Anything new is always a leap of faith; it's not just social. When the internet first became a thing, there will have been people putting a business case together to justify why they needed a website. Now it would be unthinkable not to have a web presence. Social's turn will come when it is so accepted that you won't have to go through this process. But that might be a little way off yet, so you may need to play the numbers game.

There are measures of course. You can measure influence, through tools like **Klout** or Social Mention (one of us was asked at a recent conference to explain what Klout was as the MD had added it to their monthly performance KPIs - but no-one in the company had any idea what it was!). You can use Google Analytics to see whether your social activity is driving your customers to your website and then converting into any action you want them to take, from leaving their email address to making a purchase. Google Analytics can tell you where your visitors are coming from and where they go.

One of the challenges however is attribution. Sometimes you will be able to tell whether a customer has completed a purchase or an action by the data, but not always. If someone has just become aware of your brand over time through your social efforts, and then becomes a customer, this won't be easy to track.

You can measure exposure and reach by looking at blog views, comments, likes and shares – essentially identifying how many people have engaged with your stuff. Sites like TweetReach can tell you how far your tweet travelled. Twitter itself now has an analytics function you can see for your own profile. You can measure follower numbers and track overall growth, whatever platform you are on. You can track leads from social feeds.

There are specific tools that you can use that will do some measurement on your behalf. Some are free and some are paid or **freemium**. As with most things, you will get a little more with the paid for versions or upgrades in terms of functionality.

The problem is that when it comes to measurement, you can focus a little too much on how many likes a post got, or the favourites, comments and retweets. Again, this tells you something, but not everything.

Also relevant to the ROI question is **search engine optimisation** (SEO). Social media such as blogging or YouTube video, or other people linking to your social content is good for the SEO of your main corporate website, make you a higher authority. It can drive you traffic. To some extent, what you do online is more easily tracked than more traditional forms of marketing. You can monitor that traffic. Which of your social sharing has driven it to your site? How long did they stay? How did they move around? Did they actually do anything that you wanted them to do, like give you their email address, or actually buy something?

When you are making your business case, here are some other points to consider:

- It might be stating the obvious, but link your return on investment to your goals. Whether that is driving sales, increasing brand awareness, helping with recruitment, link them together.

- When it comes to considering what the investment should be, remember that social is not free. It is not even cheap. But it can be significantly cheaper than other forms of marketing, and deliver a more long term value. Take an event. You can pay a lot of money for a stand. Even more money for the event literature. And then there are all the free pens and mugs to give away. When it is done, and all the branded sweets have been eaten, it is done. It existed, for the most part, for those few days. A similar investment in social lives longer.

- Social media is not about short term sales increases or quick wins. It is a long term game. Because you are building a long term relationship, not having a one-night stand. When people go on a social media site, they primarily go on for social reasons. To share a photograph, read what others have posted, chat to a friend. As a general rule, when it comes to finding your stuff people will find it by chance, because their friends chat about it or engage with it. Measuring this kind of activity in any meaningful way is very difficult. So maybe just focus on the content – but the test should be does the content help build your brand, not will the content get likes. Anyone can write a **clickbait** headline, but there has to be some substance beneath it.

- Consider why people will follow your brand or organisation. It might be that they are looking for a job at your place- because they also work in your industry or you share interesting stuff.

- Build in a review cycle. Goals, activity, outcomes, review. Measuring ROI is an ongoing thing – a cycle. Keep your approach and activities under constant review.

- Make sure you are listening too, about what is being said about your brand in the social space. There are plenty of tools that you can use for this – and make sure that you respond to people quickly, especially if they contact you directly via social media.

Above all, when it comes to social return on investment, the only thing that will get people following you, engaging you, sharing your stuff, is providing them with interesting, relevant content. Without that, you will get almost no return at all.

So if you can, if you work at that sort of place, maybe not getting hung up on the numbers is best. It will deliver. But it will take time. And then one day it will just be accepted as a necessity, just like your website. Or your Mum.

As one of our favourite social media gurus, Erik Qualman, wrote, "The return on investment [in social] is that your business will still exist in five years."

Rule Number Six

Check out the competition

Find and/or follow your competitors and see what they are doing on social media. Where they are, what sort of content they share, and how successful they appear to be. How many followers do they have, how often are they sharing, what hashtags are they using? This will help you understand more about what you need to do to get one better! You might also learn some valuable information and techniques along the way.

Don't be afraid to follow them. The worst they can do is block you.

#Facepalm – how to avoid getting it wrong

There are horror stories everywhere about social media. You may have heard about the girl who befriended her boss on Facebook, and then complained about the tasks she was doing and described that same manager in her status as 'pervy'. He dismissed her via the comments section. Then there was the example of the employee who, before getting on a long haul flight for a business trip to Africa, made a highly inappropriate comment on Twitter about AIDS and race. The tweet went viral, and the hashtag #hasjustinelandedyet was trending worldwide. Her employers had issued a statement confirming her dismissal before the plane touched down. Only recently an employee in the US was fired before even starting her new job, having posted a status update complaining about the job and the company in colourful language.

So here are some thoughts from us, on not making a social media fail – personally or professionally.

1. Don't just give it to kids. Someone once suggested to us that they could "get an apprentice" to manage the corporate social media accounts, based on what appeared only to be the assumption that the kids know how to do this stuff. Do you really want to hand over your brand to an inexperienced teenager straight out of school? Thought not. Bear in mind the now-infamous HMV story from 2013 where a significant number of staff were being made redundant and the whole thing was live-tweeted on the company's official Twitter feed, using the hashtag #hmvXFactorFiring. One of the tweets memorably quoted the Marketing Director as asking "How do I shut down Twitter?" because the account had been set up by an intern and no-one else knew what the password was.

2. Respond to your customers, quickly and respectfully. If your customers send you a tweet, especially a negative one, then deal with it. Monitor your accounts, always. Take the discussion offline if you have to but if you can resolve it quickly and painlessly, you will benefit from the positive PR. Trust us, we've seen it happen.

3. Don't try and be on every platform all the time. You couldn't do all of them well even if you tried and even if you employed a huge team whose sole job was just to do it. It's far better to target specific sites that work for you. For most organisations, that's Facebook and Twitter. However, one local artisan bakery we know of makes extensive use of Instagram – filling their followers' timelines with frankly irresistible images of fresh cakes and bread that can drive you crazy...

4. Train the people you worth with. We have said it elsewhere in this book. You do need to help people, both with the practical how to, the etiquette of social, but also what not to do. Show them our suggested social accounts to follow. Let them spend some time watching what goes on with successful social media users. One of the recent cases to make it through the employment tribunal system involved an employee dismissed for tweeting inappropriately. A close read of the detail makes it obvious that the employee didn't really know what he was doing on the network. When challenged, he had asked his 14 year old son to help him delete the offending tweets. Enough said.

5. Don't buy followers or likes. It is obvious to anyone who understands social media and makes you look like you don't know what you are doing. If your content is interesting enough, you will get real ones, even if it takes a bit of time. If you try to short circuit the system, you're just missing the point.

6. Things we (and pretty much everyone else too) really hate: automated Direct Messages on Twitter – they do not, repeat not, engage anyone. Facebook pages that are never updated, or worse still are updated with meaningless corporate nonsense every 5 minutes. Blank LinkedIn connection requests that don't say why the person wants to link in with you. And when you accept one, an immediate email suggesting you buy their products. Try not to do any of these things.

7. Oversharing your stuff. It is the equivalent of running around shouting 'we are awesome' in a very loud voice at everyone. Social media is not a one-way broadcast channel so you

shouldn't treat it like one. Share other people's stuff, be useful, be chatty. People on social media respond to seeing others showing a bit of character rather than just issuing bland corporate statements all the time.

8. Not being 24/7 if your brand is. Social isn't 9-5. Most businesses aren't either. Public Relations issues don't always arise during normal office hours. Make sure you keep the content coming, and you have a plan for dealing with issues that arise when your social media manager isn't at his or her desk.

9. Not selling, selling, selling. Don't ram your products and services down people's throats. They will just unfollow you or disconnect with you. Be instead, a useful social human.

As a general rule, behave like you would in real life. If a customer came into your shop with a complaint, you would attend to them and try to resolve it as quickly and as peacefully as possible. If you met someone at a networking event, you wouldn't immediately start lecturing them about how wonderful your product was at the handshake. If someone talks to you, then usually you will talk back and establish a frame of reference and how you might be of mutual benefit.

Giving it a Go

We hope that our book has inspired you to get a little social, or encourage your organisation to do the same. When it comes to getting stuck in for yourself, we have three simple recommendations.

- Be You
- Dive In
- Share Stuff

Be You. On social media just be yourself (unless of course you are a total arse, in which case be nicer). Be authentic. People will know if you are not. Be open and honest to people. We have often met people first in a social world, and then gone on to meet them **IRL** (in real life). We have learnt one important thing; people face to face are often very much like they are in the virtual world. If people do nothing but blatant self-promotion on Twitter, they are usually just like that at a networking event.

Dive In. There are plenty of people who just watch on Twitter. Lurking is the official term. That is absolutely fine. But you will get the most out of it by getting involved and actively participating. People often respond with 'but I don't know what to say'. Our answer is simple: a tweet has a shelf life of maybe 30 minutes max, so just go for it. If you say something daft, chances are only a few people will notice it anyway. Just be brave (and exercise some common sense). Don't worry about crafting something profound. Tweet like no one is watching (apart from your mother).

Share Stuff. Everything like someone who shares their stuff. It is the best way to make new connections. People also like to follow people or connect with people who find interesting articles and pass them on through their networks. There are however plenty of folk around who just share their own stuff and nothing else. The minute you accept their LinkedIn connection they start sending you spam about why you should do business with them. You may want to avoid these people.

In return for giving it a go, we have some promises to make you.

- It is welcoming
- It is full of learning
- It is fun
- You can find out lots about One Direction (Note from Tim – it is most definitely just Gemma that is interested in this).

As we said. There are no rules. But there is some etiquette. This is pretty simple too. Acknowledge your sources when sharing stuff. Say thank you when people share yours. Be polite. Humour is fine but stay away from bad taste. Try not to argue with trolls or unpleasant individuals; you will just waste your energy. Don't try to sell someone your product the first time you engage with them.

Just like the rules for a face to face meeting really.

Myth Busting

We find that when we meet people who know that we are self-confessed social media addicts, we get asked lots of the same questions and are on the receiving end of lots of the same comments. And typically, we give pretty much the same responses. If you start to get social either professionally, personally, or indeed both, then we reckon you will get these questions too. So here are our responses, to save you the time.

How do you find the time?

The answer to this one is simple. If you want to do something enough, then you will find a way and make the time. And as the saying goes, if you don't, you will find an excuse. That is why there are usually more people down the pub than in the gym.

I know I should give it a go.

Usually said in the same tone of voice we use when we ponder tackling our household chores. See the above comment. Here's the thing – if you are thinking about getting social, you have to know why you are doing it. Because if you don't have a good why, an aim, then you will find it hard to be motivated to get going or keep going. Our why is simple. We use social media to learn from others, to make great connections, to chat to friends and to get updates on One Direction (Note from Tim – just to remind you, that last one is just Gemma).

Isn't Twitter just about people saying what they had for breakfast?

No.

I don't know what to say.

Don't worry about it too much. You manage to have conversations with people at work all day right? You are not crafting a novel. Just stay away from the obvious inflammatory stuff. If you worry about it or overthink it, you will never do it.

How do you cope with the constant stream of stuff coming at you?

Cognitive overload is a real thing. And it's not just about social media. Emails, phone calls, text messages, voicemails, instant messages, alerts, notifications. We are constantly connected, constantly interrupted. You can find a way to manage the social stuff just like you do with the rest of it. In Twitter, you can use lists. Some people use apps or feeds for collation or to make sure they don't miss something important to them. You also have to be selective on who you follow and what you read, or you could easily be overwhelmed. You can't catch every tweet or post so don't even try – it simply isn't meant to be used that way.

I don't know how to do it. There is all this terminology that I don't understand.

It takes a little getting used to, just like anything new. But it isn't all that hard, if you want to learn it. In most areas of interest, professions, disciplines, hobbies or pursuits, there will be welcoming communities who will help you along the way. Plus you now have a handy glossary at the back of this book to help.

Isn't it a bit sad?

This all depends on your point of view. Nothing is sad if you get some benefit from it or enjoy it. Can you take it too far? Yes of course you can. There is balance in all things, including social media. But to us there is nothing sad about learning, reading, collaborating or chatting to our friends.

Isn't it just for the younger generation?

Nope. It is true that the younger you are, the more you have grown up with this stuff, the more it is second nature. For those currently at school, there was no time before the internet or the mobile phone. But writing it off as something for those pesky kids is both dangerous and inaccurate. The evidence points to the fact that it simply isn't the case and in the case of some social media platforms, the fastest growing demographic is the older generation. It looks like you can teach an old dog new tweets.

It doesn't apply to us / me / our business.

Whether we like it or not, believe it or not, social is the new normal. This is the world that we live in, today and tomorrow. It isn't going anywhere. The individual platforms might come and go, trends will rise and fall, but we now live in a mobile, connected, digital world. Your customers are there, your potential customers are there, your employees are there, and your friends are there. You can choose if you want to be there too. And it is a choice. But there are risks with not engaging too.

If you have any more questions, just look us up on Twitter (you can find us at @HR_Gem and @TimScottHR, remember!) and tweet us.

Rule Number Seven

Be interesting

Now we have mentioned this elsewhere in this book. But this is so important (and so many people get it wrong) that we thought it deserved a whole section to itself.

We both follow brands in our social feeds. Sometimes, we are already a customer of that brand. Sometimes, we just like the cut of their jib. If you are interesting and a useful resource, then people will follow you, even if they don't choose to interact immediately in the form of buying one of your products or services. That is just fine. Because, when they do need something in your space, you will be at the forefront of their mind.

So how do you do this?

First of all, don't scream constantly about your products and services. Don't do the hard sell, especially early on. There is little we dislike more than accepting a LinkedIn connection request and a few minutes getting an email to 'introduce themselves'. Which basically means try and sell you something. Or connecting with someone and then being subjected to a stream of self-promoting posts. And we know we're not alone in these dislikes.

As an absolute maximum, you should not mention your products or services more than once in every five social shares. Maximum. One in ten would be better to be honest. It is hugely important to strike a balance – and that balance needs to be weighted heavily in favour of the "being interesting and useful" stuff, to the 'let me tell you about what I do' stuff.

If you consistently share content, from multiple sources and of multiple types, to your audience, then you are a valuable account / individual to engage with. This helps you establish credibility as a source and helps you build trust with your audience.

Here are some other ideas to help you be interesting and useful:

- Don't forget images. An image always increases engagement and makes your post more eye catching.

- Get some dialogue going. Maybe it's a poll on Twitter. It could be posing a question for comments, or contributing to one that is already happening in a relevant group.

- Competitions. Don't overlook the value of a freebie. If you a Personal Trainer, they try getting people to re-tweet for the chance to win a free consultation. If you are a cake decorator, share or like for a free cake delivered to the office. And so on. You get the message. This will help be remembered, but will also get you shared and into other peoples' social feeds.

- Share your knowledge and ideas. Chances are, whatever it is you do, you know something that others don't, or would find interesting. Maybe write a blog post with some top tips.

- Make it seasonal. Without going overboard, align your stuff to the time of year. Holidays, national events and the like give great opportunities to tailor or share something relevant and interesting.

- Share often. Keep it up if you want to keep people engaged.

Here are some of our suggestions of stuff not to do:

- Don't automate too much stuff. Tools like **TweetDeck** can save you time and effort, but you can often tell when something is scheduled. If you do use scheduling, make sure you have the ability to turn it off, quickly. For example, in the wake of a natural disaster, it won't do your business any favours if you are sending automated light-hearted tweets. Also, turn automated stuff off at Christmas. No one wants to pop onto Twitter to wish everyone a Happy Christmas on Christmas Day morning and see automated adverts for business products and services.

- Never auto **DM** anyone through Twitter when they follow you. It's annoying.

- It's fine to share the same thing across different social media channels, although it might need some tailoring. But try not to do it at the same time. If someone is following you in more than once social space, they don't want to see the same content from you multiple times, all at once. You run the risk that they will disengage with you in one of those places.

Picking Your Platforms

As we said earlier, there are many, many forms of social media, and it is a developing space.

We can't cover them all in this book, and neither can you.

Our advice is always the same. Pick a couple of platforms that suit your business, and do them really well. Over the next few pages, we are going to take a few of the options and go into a bit more detail on the as well as some tips and things to think about when deciding which ones to do. The big platforms that you should be considering, and give you some ideas on how to do each. Note, this is the biggest chapter. You might want to get a cup of team before beginning this one.

Twitter

We are big advocates of Twitter. If we were to suggest that there is a platform that you definitely should be on, it is this one. A quick recap – Twitter is about sharing stuff that is no more than 140 characters. You can include images or links in your tweets. Its aim is to share stuff that is short and sharp. There are businesses of all shapes and sizes on Twitter. In fact, it is really unusual to find a business that is not on Twitter today.

Top Tips for Twitter:

- Tweets do not have a long life, as most people just don't scroll too far back in their timelines. So tweet regularly. If you can't be on the platform often enough, you can schedule tweets to go out at set times, for example through an app called **TweetDeck** or Hootsuite. So you will need to be tweeting often – at least several times a day

- Mix it up. Tweet links and images. Don't just tweet your own stuff, share from others too. (We will be saying this a lot)

- Engage. Include other users (sparingly!) by tagging them in your tweets by typing "@username" – this means you can engage directly with them as your tweet will appear in their notifications not just their timeline

- Use **hashtag**s. You can make up your own, or check out what relevant ones already exist that are relevant to you. You don't have to do anything to set up a hashtag, you simply type it. You can even create one just for your business if you want. Just a reminder: you can't put spaces or punctuation in a hashtag and it is worth thinking carefully about how some words look when they are all run together. There have been some pretty comic hashtag fails over the years

- Re-tweet other people as a way of engaging with them

LinkedIn

The professional networking site. Like many sites, it has a 'freemium' model, which means that there is stuff that you can get for free, and other additional stuff that you can pay for. For example on LinkedIn, you can pay for an enhanced profile or job advertising.

There are two board options on LinkedIn. One is to have a personal profile, the other is to have a company profile. For the small business or self-employed practitioner, we recommend just having a really good personal profile.

Company pages are great, but the free ones are very limited in terms of what you can do on them apart from sharing updates. There is an option to have a paid-for company page

Top Tips for LinkedIn

- Have a complete profile – including a professional headshot. This is not the place for wedding photos, car pictures or cropped photos from a night out. A proper photograph is an investment, so have one taken if you don't already have one. At the very least, get someone to take a photo of you against a plain background and with you looking vaguely like you might be about to do a day's work. As for the wider profile, LinkedIn will prompt and guide you on what areas need to be completed.

- Get recommendations for your work. Recommendations are hugely important. They are a visible testimonial and reasons why people should choose to work with you and your business. Don't be afraid to ask people to write one. The worst thing that they can do is ignore you!

- Keep it professional! There are people who seriously confuse LinkedIn with other, less formal sites. Don't post memes, personal stuff, pictures of lottery tickets and the like. You will just become annoying and people might choose to disengage with you entirely.

- Don't spam people! This is another big problem with the platform in our opinion. You connect with someone and then they start adding you to their mailing list or sending you links to their products straight away.

- Do join groups, and take part in discussions. This is a good way to build new connections and increase visibility of your profile.

- As with all the platforms, as well as sharing your own stuff, share other people's too.

Facebook

The most commonly used platform still. It has now reached a stage where if all the members of Facebook were the population of a country, it would be the most populous in the world. So not a bad place to be thinking about building your personal or company profile. Facebook is generally more informal than other networks. It isn't really the sort of place that you go looking for products, businesses and suppliers. For the most part, people go there to chat to friends, keep in touch, share pictures and the like. Users are more likely to stumble upon something or someone, unless we are talking about promoted posts. You will often find, in the middle of your feed or along the side on a desktop, products and services that you might be interested in. Often, they are just the things that you have been looking at over on your Amazon or eBay accounts. They will be paid-for adverts, following you around the web based on your previous searches. You can have these too but they can be super expensive.

Top Tips for Facebook:

- As we have included in one of our rules – never mix up your personal and professional Facebook profiles! Your clients do not want to see your baby photos.

- Facebook has algorithms that choose what people see in their feed. So you can't guarantee that your post will be seen by your followers, so regularity is important here too.

- Engage with your followers. This might just be responding to comments, but also consider posting a question or a poll to get people talking to you. Depending on how their privacy settings are organised, this should mean that you are seen in the feeds of the friends of your followers.

- You can use Facebook's own tools to analyse when your followers are active on the platform, so you can target your posts accordingly.

- Mix it up in order to grow your followers. Don't just do text posts, include videos, pictures and links.

- Facebook Live is a relatively new feature which lets you broadcast video direct from your device to the world via Facebook in competition with Periscope. Video is already massive on the internet as technology and internet speeds continue to improve exponentially. Done well, it offers businesses massive opportunities to showcase their products and services.

Instagram

Instagram is an image sharing site for photos and video. Images are great as they often get more interaction than plain old text posts. Images can tell a story about your organisation, as well as showcase your products and services.

With one additional click you can also share them straight onto other platforms. Instagram is great for any business, but will be particularly good for anyone with a very visual product: think food, clothing, home decoration and the like. You can also share pictures and video of your people or your premises.

Top Tips for Instagram:

- Post at least once a day

- Use the filters that are available in the App to improve the pictures – just play around, it is quite user friendly

- Engage with people that comment on your photos – reply and follow them back

- Link Instagram up to your other accounts like Facebook or Twitter to share on multiple platforms all at once

- Use humour and fun in your images, it will get good engagement and give your brand a personality

- Have a good profile and bio (applies to most of these sites!)

Pinterest

The easiest way to think about Pinterest is like a big online notice board. It is image-based, with the ability to share links and videos too. Users create 'boards' on which they 'pin' images that they like or want to share.

There are Pinterest boards for pretty much everything. From wedding dresses to health and fitness. From recipes to tattoo designs. From your favourite band to motivational quotes.

Pinterest is fab for showcasing what you do, especially if it is a visual product. For example, if you run a wedding business, you could have a board showing wedding dresses, another for flowers and another for bridesmaid outfits. If you are a photographer, you could show samples of your work. If you are a small business, you could show pictures of your premises and your team.

The benefit of Pinterest is that it is very easy to take a photograph on your phone, and upload it to the platform. You can put a link to the boards on your website, or simply occasionally tweet links to it.... 'Check out our Pinterest Boards here for more images of our products'.

You don't necessarily need to worry about building a following, because you can just direct people to the site for a good look around at any point in time.

Top Tips for Pinterest:

- Organise your content into easily understood 'boards'

- Unless you are pinning a heck of a lot, you might find it hard to get followers just based on your feed. You might be best thinking of Pinterest as a showcase that you can direct people too

- Follow other people – they might just follow you back!

- Keep your eye on interactions – you will find a 'you' section as well as a 'messages' section. The 'you' will show you anyone who has saved or liked your pins. The messages are, as indicated, messages directly to you from other pinners

- This is one site where you want to concentrate on sharing your own stuff, rather than other people's. Firstly, you don't always know the source or copyright of images on somewhere like Pinterest, and you don't want to get yourself in legal hot water. But as per the point above – because this is a primarily image site, this is a place to showcase your work, not someone else's

- Make sure you put descriptions on your pins to say exactly what they are. Also add a web link that will take people straight to your website

- Get creative with your images! There are fun and cheap apps that you can use to put text over your pictures. Try Wordswag as a simple to use option

YouTube

You might not always think of YouTube as social media. It is the second most-used search engine in the world and also features heavily in Google search results. But it is also a social platform in that it allows people to share from it and comment on posts. Getting videos on

YouTube could be a real opportunity depending on the type of business you run. You can set up your own You Tube channel for free and include your own branding. It is great for visual content and the beauty is that whatever you share on YouTube can also be shared easily across your other platforms.

Options could include: putting clips of you presenting or at work, videos of your shop premises, or your products being manufactured, "A day in the life"-type posts or a demonstration of what you are offering. It doesn't hurt to give something away via social media. So if you run a cake business, put a video up on how to make a cake. Personal Trainer? Try a few short videos of how to do some exercise in your own home. If people engage with you and follow your channel, you will remain in their mind when they are ready to spend some money.

Top Tips for YouTube:

- Keep it short to ensure that viewers don't disengage part way through your video

- Name and describe your videos well, so that they will show up in organic search results, not just people who get referred from your other feeds

- You can pay to have professional videos shot and edited. But this might prove too expensive. So you can do your own, if you own a reasonable video camera. Don't forget most smartphones these days will shoot video in HD and the video is only likely to be viewed on the same sized screen – it doesn't have to IMAX 3D! It is okay to talk straight to camera for something like a vlog

- There is so much content uploaded to YouTube every day that you might not get high views with addition promotion. So share your video links everywhere!

- Make sure you use your brand logo on the site (same goes for all platforms really!)

- Don't add music unless you have permission – or it is copyright-free

- If you go onto YouTube itself, there are step by step tutorials on how to upload content and create your own channel

Snapchat

The idea behind Snapchat is to share images that are short-lived – both pictures and videos. Once seen, they disappear. Videos last up to 10 seconds in length, and then disappear after a single viewing. Said to have 150 million active daily users. Still overall something of a niche platform with a much younger demographic – but growing quickly. Definitely a platform to watch for the future.

How to decide….

When it comes to deciding which of these platforms to focus on, the single most important question is….. *Where are your customers?* What are the social media networks that they are using? You may be able to research this, by asking existing customers or friends and family. Some Google searching might also give you some pointers. Or you simply might need to experiment for a while to see what gives you the best results and adapt accordingly.

We do know this: unless you have a marketing department, you probably can't do all of them really well. So pick a couple (most brands have two or more social media channels) and put effort into those.

A few facts that might help you decide:

- Instagram and Pinterest work best for brands and businesses with very visual content. Pizza is the most Instagrammed food! Instagram is cited by one third of teens to be their favourite network.

- The best time to Pin to Pinterest is Saturday evening. Used to be a female dominated network but the male audience is growing quickly.

- Facebook is still the biggest platform in the world – and it still continues to grow. The average user has over 300 friends. There are 40 million active small business pages.

- Twitter users typically expect a response from a brand that they tweet within one hour. Over two thirds of people say that they feel more positive about a brand when their tweet is replied to and there are 6000 tweets sent every second!

- Snapchat is the third most popular app amongst 18-34 year olds (still behind Facebook and Instagram but growing fast).

- LinkedIn has over 450 million users worldwide. 2 new people join the network every second. Important in the business to business space.

- Video is important – wherever you are uploading it. 78% of internet users watch online video every week.

Whichever you go with, be prepared to change. Networks rise and fall in popularity (anyone remember MySpace?) and demographics change too, not to mention new platforms arriving regularly. So keep up with the trends!

And finally…. whichever platform you choose, make sure that you are sharing and updating regularly. There is nothing worse than an abandoned social profile – arguably with the sole exception of not having one at all!

Blogs

We fell that this area is so important we have given it its own chapter.

There are several different platforms in which you can set up a blog. Probably the most common is **WordPress**, and it is very user friendly. You don't need any specialist design skills to get one up and running and they have a help function if you get stuck.

First things first. Why would you blog?

We are BIG advocates of blogging. It makes you think. It makes you creative. It improves your communication skills. But above anything, it is <u>great</u> for your business brand. It establishes your authority as someone who knows what they are talking about and has knowledge in your own particular professional space. And you do. Otherwise you wouldn't be running this business. Even if something feels pretty standard to you, there will be people out there who don't know much about it and will be interested in what you have to say.

The upside of blogging is how easy it is to get started. It is good for generating traffic to your website, and can be used to demonstrate to clients your areas of expertise. It gives you something to share on the other social media platforms that you are using to promote your business. Blogging also tells a story. It is more in-depth than the quick interactions of somewhere like Twitter (although that is an excellent place to link to your blog). Blogging can give your brand a personality beyond a bland corporate website.

The downside is that it takes a little time to get the posts written and you will need to keep at it to get regular readers. It will take time to build, so keep at it.

There are some practical things to think about when blogging. Although there are free sites out there, some, like WordPress, have paid for features. For example, you can pay to have your own domain name (otherwise, you will have something like thenameofyourblog@wordpress.com. Instead, you can have thenameofyourblog.com. It is a small difference but does look a bit more professional. Also on WordPress, some visitors to your site will get adverts at the bottom of your posts. You can pay an annual fee to have an advert-free site. Both of these cost relatively little. You can also pay for better graphics and layouts, but this is a personal choice and style thing. We definitely recommend paying for the no adverts option. It is less than about £30 per year, and we feel it is better to spend that than risk finding yourself with dodgy adverts on your professional site.

Overall, as marketing goes, once you take into account the costs plus the potential benefits, blogging is a very cost effective method of getting your message out there.

Our top tips for blogging:

- Think about when you are posting content. When you have written a few posts, you will be able to go onto the analytics page and see when people are visiting your side, or what posts are most popular. You should be aiming for at least a post per week.

- Include images within your posts, as this will typically get you more engagement, but be very careful not to breach copyright! You can of course use your own photos or look out for royalty free images.

- A good length for a post is 400-500 words. Keep the subject to one central theme.

- Make sure that there are sharing buttons on your posts, so that your readers can easily share them on social media. Allow readers to post comments too so that you can get a conversation going. Always reply to your comments!

- Be timely. People will engage with posts that are relevant to them but also relevant to what is going on at the time. For example, if you are in the health business, then January is the time of year that everyone goes on a diet – so make sure your posts make the most of it! Also think about the holidays, festivals and occasions that mean something to your business – for example, Valentine's Day, Eid, Summer Holidays, Halloween, Diwali, Thanksgiving, Hanukkah, Christmas…

- The title of your post is hugely important. It is the difference between someone clicking on the link or simply scrolling past. So create good titles. List posts are good (e.g. 5 ways to achieve this, that or the other) but can get a bit repetitive so mix it up. Make sure your title says what is on the tin – so people get what they expected when they click.

- Make sure that people can sign up by email to get your future posts – this is normally just a widget that you can simply add in from your settings menu. This makes sure that when you publish a new post, it is also dropping into the inbox of your regular readers.

- Give your overall blog a relevant name that clearly explains what they posts within will be about. It might simply be the name of your business, if that works. For example, one of Gem's blogs is called simply 'People Stuff', because she writes about things that relate to people at work.

Finding stuff to share

As we have said elsewhere in this book, one of the big barriers to getting social in the early days for many people is actually knowing what to share.

What you definitely don't want to do, is constantly share only your own stuff. Firstly, it makes you look a bit like you are very impressed with yourself. And secondly, sharing other people's stuff is a really great way to make contacts and expand your network. Everyone automatically loves someone who shares their stuff, especially if you add a brief comment like "Great post from @username on x, y and z".

It is a good idea to have something of a strategy about what you will share. It doesn't need to be a complicated strategy or even written down. If your Twitter bio describes you as an IT professional, but you are spending all of your time tweeting about football, then this is only going to confuse your followers. Or worse, make them unfollow you. So if you are an IT professional looking to engage with other IT people, ensure you tweet at least some IT stuff – your own or other people's. Switch the football chat to a private or personal account.

There are a few ways that you can collate good information to share with your network. Mostly you will find that articles and things of interest will land naturally in your timeline because of the people you follow on each platform. Depending on how many and what kind of people or accounts you follow, you may find the vast majority – or even all – of the content you share there.

There are also apps that can help you find content from across the web. There are a number that do this, for example scoop.it. You input your areas of interest, and it will collate articles and blog posts from across the net. There are also apps like 'Pocket' to which you can save articles when you come across them for later reading and/or sharing. Some people use Evernote or Pinterest to do it too (this works just fine as long as the post has a picture associated with it. If it all sounds a little complicated don't worry: these apps are designed to be easy to use and you will get used to them after a little practice.

Over on Twitter there is a "Moments" tab that tells you the latest news. There is also an area that tells you what is **trending** – you can change this to worldwide or local trends. If a subject that is of interest or relevance to your business is trending, it may indicate that it's a good time for you to search the hashtag or publish something of your own using that hashtag.

Many business writers publish their articles on LinkedIn and given its professional focus, it can be a great place to find relevant content for your areas of interest. Beware of the quality though as many, despite high share counts, are click bait.

Rule Number Eight

Listen

Social is a two-way dialogue. That means it isn't just about broadcasting or selling, but listening too. Social listening is all about tuning in to what people are saying, whether that is specifically about your organisation or brand, or more generally about your industry, to influencers, to what your competitors are doing or talking about.

There are tools that help you listen.

One of the simplest that will work for most people is probably Google Alerts. You simply go to www.google.com/alerts and set up what search terms you want to be alerted to. For example, you could include your own name or the name of your company. You could also set up terms that relate to what you do – be specific though or it might drive you crazy.

Once you have set up alert, Google will let you know by email when relevant new content, based on your settings, is posted online. You control how often you want to receive these alerts. So if someone is talking about you or your brand online, you will be able to find out and respond.

If you want to get a little more specific, there are tools that allow you to monitor what people are saying about you on social media – some charge, but also offer free trials or a basic account for gratis. Check out Mention and Social Mention as two easy to use options. There are plenty more though if you don't like those. Simply search 'social media listening tools' and you will find links aplenty.

The Marketing Mix

It's time to revisit what we talked about in Rule Number One.

If you have ever been on a marketing course, you will have heard this term. It has been around for decades. The 'four Ps' were probably covered on that same course; product, place, promotion and price. The model has been played around with and added to over the years, and for the digital age, some additional Ps were added too: people, personalise, participate.

When it comes to marketing mix, we mean something a little different. For the purposes of this little book, we mean the mix of marketing that you need to do to sell your products and services.

Every so often, someone comes along and declares something or other officially dead. Email is a good example. Whilst many people dislike email (or rather its impact upon them and the way that some people choose to use it), despite all the plethora of social channels, its use isn't declining. Far from it. And whilst social media presents opportunities to network in all new ways, neither is the need to get out and meet people **IRL**.

So what we are saying is that social is just part of how you sell your business or what you do. A very important part – an increasingly important part, we would argue – but it can't be everything for many reasons. As much as we are social types and are encouraging you to be the same, there are some people who don't use it at all, for a whole variety of reasons. Focusing entirely on social will limit your opportunities, which isn't helpful to anyone.

So our advice is simple. Mix it up and take opportunities to bring online and offline together. In other words, use your social media activity to drive people to your traditional marketing methods (where appropriate) and vice versa.

So, if you send out an email bulletin or the like from time to time (you should you know, it's a great way to keep in touch with customers and potential customers alike and remain top of mind) then make sure you include links to all of your social feeds and an easy invitation to follow you there.

You do have some business cards, don't you? Yes, we know that you can look someone up on LinkedIn any time you like, but a business card is still a handy tool to have when you meet people for the first time. And just the same as above, make sure your business card signposts how to follow you on Twitter, the address of your blog and so on.

How does your website look? Once upon a time, everyone was in the Phone Book. These days it is almost unthinkable that you would try and run a business without a website. Social media will be like that in the future and this book will be obsolete, which is just fine with us. The advice is the same. Promote your social feeds on your website. And use your social feeds to promote your website. Include links to it in your tweets and blogs and posts.

Hard copy stuff like brochures, leaflets and the like are all good things to have, even in the social and digital world. In the next chapter, there's a great example of how to do this really well. So keep doing it, but just as we said above, make sure that these things are pointing people in the direction of your social feeds too.

Face to face networking is still important - in other words, actually being social. The original social, perhaps, it's still relevant, still important. When you've met someone IRL, make sure that you find them on LinkedIn and send them a connection request. Find them on Twitter and say hi. Give them a business card with your details on. You already know the drill.

A Very Important P

As we said on the previous page, the traditional view of the marketing mix is price, promotion, place and product. You could head over to that social font of all knowledge Wikipedia for more information on that.

One very important P when it comes to all things social is promotion. Promote your products and services to others of course, but get creative too. It's really easy to run simple competitions and giveaways for example.

- *Like this Facebook page for the chance to win a freebie* (because someone likes your page, you will keep showing up in their feed)

- *Re-tweet this tweet to enter into a prize draw* (because then your tweet bounces into the timelines of your followers' followers)

And don't forget to follow up the winning individual. During a conference at which we were speaking, we gave away a copy of our last book as a "prize" for sending the best tweet in the session. And then took a picture of us giving it away and tweeted it!

Don't be afraid of adding 'please re-tweet' in a tweet (or RT for short). Evidence shows that lots of people will do as they are asked.

So get creative!

Social Media That Rocks

Still stuck for ideas after all this stuff?

If you need a little inspiration, here are just a few of our favourite UK-based social media feeds that rock. Most of the brands listed below have a strong presence on both Facebook and Twitter as they are the main sites to engage with consumers.

Innocent Drinks

Funny and engaging across multiple platforms. Check out their Twitter feeds and Instagram accounts in particular. They combine relevant, witty original content with good, responsive customer service. Like each of the brands mentioned below, they are worth following whether you are a consumer of their products or not – meaning that their brand is being reinforced all the time. A true social brand.

Virgin Trains

Arguably an unlikely candidate to do social media well, Virgin Trains use Twitter to inject some humour and personality when responding to the mundane customer queries ("What time is the next train from x to y?" etc.) and dealing with the inevitable complaints about delays or cancellations. One of us may once have played online I-Spy with them when bored on a train journey.

GiffGaff

Another highly responsive Twitter account that mixes fun and interesting tweets with effective customer responses and interaction. GiffGaff are an alternative mobile phone provider so you'd kind of expect them to "get" social media but they do it with style.

Tesco

Believe it or not, the UK's largest supermarket retailer has a fun and chatty approach to social media in sharp contrast to a number of other big brands. It has occasionally got them into hot water but we think it's worth the risk to interact with customers as successfully as they usually do.

Investors in People UK

The best example we have seen for a while on how to do social from an event. Their Twitter feeds from HR conferences are great, sharing real time quotes and graphics. They really know how to bring the real life stuff and the online stuff together, which is a rare skill. If you want to know how to do an event socially, even if you aren't in HR, this is the account to follow. Tweeting from events is a good way to build followers and makes you an interesting and useful person to follow. Try it!

Now some of these are pretty large companies, who probably have a whole team of people looking after their social stuff, so it's perhaps no surprise to find some good practice examples. However, there are plenty of smaller organisations and some entirely sole practitioners who are doing awesome stuff in this space too.

Here are a few of our favourites with their Twitter handles for starters.

Simon Heath – also known as @SimonHeath1

Simon is a consulting artist. He designed the cover for this very book. We came across Simon on Twitter. He tweets and blogs, and this is how most of his work comes to him. We've both engaged him in projects within organisations we have worked for, from designing producing animated induction videos to live drawing conferences. When he completes work for organisations, he shares it on his social platform. His work really is word of mouth on steroids (one of other ways that we have seen social media described!).

Thorpe Park Hotel - @ThorpeParkHotel

This is a hotel in Leeds that came to our attention when Gemma used them for a work meeting. Their Twitter feed is a good example of appealing to a broad audience (they send tweets that will appeal to guests, business delegates and people who like to eat). They use images well, tweeting pictures of their pool, spa, staff in action (making cocktails usually) and their cakes and sweet treats. They share from their menu and also shout out their suppliers. They have cards dotted around the building to pick up (business card style) promoting their

Twitter and Facebook accounts. They also interact well with people that mention them.

Their Facebook feed has videos, pictures from events such as weddings and music evenings, and generally good use of imagery. A good example for anyone in the hospitality trade.

Baltic Bakehouse - @BalticBake

One of Tim's favourites. A Liverpool-based bakery and café that runs an active Twitter feed and Instagram account, sharing photos of their enormously tempting bread, cakes, coffee and lunches. A great example of how to make someone feel desperately hungry - an approach that has on many occasions led Tim to go out of his way to visit them. They also engage really well with people that tweet them – always important. They also use their accounts to engage with other artisan bread makers around the world by sharing their hints, tips - and occasionally their mistakes!

UK Wellbeing Coach - @employeehealth6

This is an employee wellbeing business that one morning was re-tweeted into Gemma's Twitter timeline. That tweet turned into a business relationship, and its founder, Andy, became the wellbeing partner at the organisation Gemma was working for at the time. Proof right there that the right tweet in the right place at the right time will get you business.

Andy uses LinkedIn, Facebook and Twitter. His Twitter feed is a good example of balance between promoting what you do and sharing other related information. One of our important lessons throughout this book is about keeping it up. Andy is a very regular sharer and poster on several platforms. If you are in someone's feed, you are in their mind the next time they need of your services.

Kingfisher Coaching - @KingfisherCoach

Run by Ian Pettigrew, Kingfisher Coaching is all about coaching and leadership development. Ian is a prolific tweeter, blogger and well…. just about every other platform you can think of. Ian makes use of a range of technologies, including podcasts.

One of Ian's areas of specialism is working with people to help them understand their strengths and building upon them. He recently started a series via his blog that is also downloadable as a podcast, where he interviews people about their strengths. It just shows that there are plenty of ways to get creative with your social media use. There isn't anything in it directly for Ian when he does this. He is simply sharing stories that might be helpful to others. However, almost as a by-product, it helps build his brand presence, highlighting one of his areas of expertise. And that is an excellent illustration of one of the things some people occasionally forget about social media – be helpful, interesting and useful. It will, over time, pay you back.

Resource - @weareresource

This is an example of a company who really know how to mix traditional marketing with social media. They are a printing business that do creative design and marketing and manage personalised mailing, as well as produce online and digital content. They often send clients cards, calendars, notebooks and the like, which are very tweetable. You will often find those that have received them take a picture and share them – so basically they are successful at getting other people to share their brand message for them. Genius. They are also known for taking Krispy Kreme donuts to client meetings, and tweeting about them too. Great imagery, plenty of humour, lots of engagement with their followers.

If after reading this book you still aren't entirely sure where to begin, then simply find some folks to follow or connect with that are on this list or in your own particular field, and just watch and learn from them (this is officially known as lurking by the way – and there is nothing wrong with that in the early days!). Take inspiration from others.

Rule Number Nine

What goes on social media, stays on social media

You can delete stuff, but this doesn't make it disappear, as many celebrities will know to their cost. Anyone can take a screen shot of what you have tweeted or shared. So take care, don't get into arguments with trolls and stupid people, don't share things without reading them first and stay away from anything like risqué jokes, bad language or something that might be offensive to your target audience.

And a quick reminder of rule number three – stay off social media when you have had a drink or four...

Final Thoughts (Almost)

We said at the start of the book that this is the social world, and it is true. This is the new normal. Social media guru Erik Qualman, who we have mentioned elsewhere in this book, says something that goes along the lines of "we no longer have a choice whether we do social media, just how well we do it". This is very true for all businesses, large and small.

Social has already had an impact on how we work, but we are only just starting to realise its full potential. The ways in which we have worked for decades will be impacted. Frankly, social blows the bloody doors off.

The truth is – we must adapt.

Because we know what happens to the organisations, functions, professions that can't, don't, or simply won't. We have all seen the case studies, the corporate corpses stinking up the joint. Even very large companies, with plenty of people paid lots of money who should have seen this stuff coming, have been taken by surprise and have paid the price. So the small business or self-employed professional has to be even more ready to spot change coming and adapt accordingly.

So to those people who say that they are not that sort of business, that they don't have those sort of customers, that they don't see that it is relevant to them, we say simply this:

Early adopter or laggard, organisations cannot put their collective heads in the sand and pretend it's not happening. Social cannot be constrained through policy and procedure, and neither can organisations afford to try to fit old solutions to these new challenges.

You can't stop it or ignore it but you can embrace it and seize the opportunities.

Let us give you an example. You may well have heard of Uber. They are the taxi company operating in several cities across the UK now. You download an app, and when you want a cab, instead of heading down to the taxi rank and standing in a queue in the cold, or attempting to wave one down in the street, you tell the app where you are and where you want to go and a taxi will soon arrive. Technology putting the consumer and the seller together. It sounds like a great idea. Only some people didn't think so – namely the black cab drivers in London. They chose to fight Uber. To take them to court and try and prevent them operating by focusing on technicalities. They didn't win. We would suggest that they would have been better spending time understanding how their world has changed, and how they could respond. You can't fight the future.

We meet people all the time who don't get social, don't like social and don't think it is relevant to them or their career or their business. They think it's just some fad that will go away. Or they tell us that they keep meaning to give it a go, in a voice that implies no interest or intent at all. We offer them these challenges:

How much space does your old black and white television set take up in your living room?

Do you long for your original, big, old Nokia mobile phone, so you can play just one more game of "Snake"?

Do you lament the lost days of the manual typewriter and the carbon copy paper?

Do you still get good value from your fax machine?

Of course not. Because the technology changed, the world moved on and we moved with it. And now it is time to move again.

This is the social world. Are you ready?

Tools and Techniques

If you run a small business, or are a stand-alone professional, then here's some useful stuff to know more about, in no particular order. That might just make things easier or more manageable.

Hoostsuite

This is a platform that can help you organise your social media accounts. To be honest, we'd suggest that this is somewhere you might want to think about going once you are really up to speed with using social.

Lists

A useful way to organise your Twitter timeline is a list. This simply means that you create lists of people and accounts, in order to organise or categorise. This means that when you want to catch up, you don't have to check back through a busy timeline, but can just select a few key areas. So for example, Gemma has a 'favetweeps' list, so that she can quickly check what her Twitter friends have been up to. Lists can either be private for your eyes only or public for the benefit of other users to see who else it might be worth following.

Scheduling Tweets

This is a way that you can schedule tweets to be sent, even when you are not around to do it yourself. There are apps to help you do this, like Hootsuite or TweetBeam among others. You write the tweets then pick the time and date(s) that you want them to go out. It is a good way to keep your presence up, perhaps when you are on holiday for example. Also, in a global world you can get a 24/7 reach – social media is the conversation that never sleeps! Some people that we follow set their previous blogs to tweet every couple of weeks. For example….. 'One from my blog archive…..' This has the benefit of making your written content useful for a long time.

Just be careful about it. For example, if there is a serious news incident or national disaster, make sure you turn them off, quickly.

Selfie

The art of taking a picture of yourself. Can be taken by hand or the popular-with-tourists selfie stick. Capable of being shared on most platforms but especially on sites like Instagram, Snapchat and Facebook. Popular with a whole host of celebs. Check out the Kardashians. If you must.

Using Hashtags

We find that people get very #confused about hashtags. First of all, don't overuse them. Second, you can just make one up. Maybe it is your #henparty. Or a #productgiveaway. Or maybe it's time for a #FridayFunny. You can search for existing hashtags in the search area of Twitter. The easiest thing to do is research them or simply see what others are using. We will probably have one for this very book. #SoMeforSMEs maybe? Some more tips in the Glossary, coming up next.

A Social Media and Technology Glossary

App

An app (short for "application") is to your mobile device as a programme is to your computer (although the word "app" is creeping into computing now too). It's the specific software that allows you to do – well, anything. Hence the phrase originally coined by Apple that "there's an app for that". There almost always is.

Blog/Blogging

A blog (the word is an abbreviation of the word "weblog") is essentially text that an author has published online. Blogs are usually informal and cover a topic of personal interest: from leadership to fitness, fashion to music. People blog about their mental health, their politics, their favourite recipes. There are sites like **Tumblr** that allow you to blog directly into their format, or you can use something like **WordPress** which allows you to build your own website around your blogging.

Click bait

Slang term for when the title of an article or blog is cunningly designed to pique the reader's curiosity and make them want to click on it to find out more. For example, "This woman slipped in the street and what happened next will amaze you". It can also be used to describe when an author has used specific popular jargon words aimed at encouraging more people to read their article. If your article is described as click bait, you can assume the describer is not intending it as a compliment...

Cloud computing

When we think of storing computer data, most of us think of the separate PC boxes we have under or on our desks which are linked together by our office network and the internet. Cloud computing is storing data on big servers remotely rather than on the individual boxes. One of the main benefits is that it can be accessed by anyone with an internet connection anywhere. If you've ever used Dropbox or Microsoft's OneDrive, you've used cloud computing.

Coffice

Slang term. Increasingly commonly in our knowledge-based economy, some types of workers aren't based in a typical office environment but are usually out and about and therefore hold meetings (or just hog the Wi-Fi) in coffee shops all over the country and generally treating public establishments as their office. So coffee shop + office = coffice.

Cognitive Assistant

The Cognitive Assistant is the next phase of development of what we used to call Artificial Intelligence (or AI) – it allows you to interact directly, usually verbally, with your technology. If you use an iPhone or iPad and have ever experienced the joy of Siri, you've used a Cognitive Assistant. Google offers Google Assistant to do a similar job. One of the benefits of using a mobile device is the use of GPS – ie they know where you are. So you can effectively treat them like personal assistants – so you could say for example "Next time I'm in the office, remind me to water the plants". Through Siri/Google Assistant your device will recognise when you are next in the location you have told it is your office and will do exactly that. Scary, eh? Amazon are now marketing the Echo as a similar system based in a smart Bluetooth speaker.

Content

In the context of the internet, content is anything that is produced and can then be shared: articles, blogs, photos, videos, presentation slide decks...

Converged devices

Remember when your mobile phone just made phone calls and that was about it? Current smartphones are so much more than just phones and can do all sorts of things with data, geo-location and other (sometimes slightly scary) technology. Mobile telephony and data – which were once chalk and cheese – have converged into one device: hence converged devices.

Crowdsourced/crowdsourcing & crowdfunding

Have you ever posted a question online like "Can anyone recommend somewhere to eat in Liverpool city centre?" Then (assuming you got some answers) you have crowdsourced. It is basically getting answers or input from a wide range of people using your online networks. You can crowdsource just about anything. TripAdvisor is a good example of crowdsourced feedback – they don't employ anyone to go out and review hotels, restaurants or attractions, they simply provide the platform to collate and co-ordinate the feedback from thousands of "ordinary" people. This kind of open feedback model is a growing area online.

Likewise there is a growth in using social technology to "crowdfund" projects, especially in the arts and music arenas. This flips the traditional music industry model - invest in album, make album, market album, hope it makes enough money to cover costs and turn a bit of profit – by getting the money needed to make the project happen first through asking fans to contribute. The fans usually get something additional in return – for example a signed copy or some other individualised merchandise that acknowledges their input. The same approach is being used to fund new products, often in the new technology market.

Visit www.kickstarter.com for more information and examples.

Enterprise Social Network/ESN

An ESN is basically just a private social network, usually restricted to one particular organisation. The big advantage of using an ESN rather than an existing network such as Twitter or Facebook is privacy: what is posted cannot be read by anyone outside of the company. This is obviously important in terms of intellectual property and competitive advantage. The most common platform is currently Microsoft's **Yammer** but everyone (well, everyone who is interested in this sort of thing) is waiting to see what the relatively new "*Workplace by Facebook*" will do to the market.

Facebook

https://www.facebook.com

The undisputed daddy of social media sites with so many users worldwide that if they all got together, they would form the most populous country in the world. Yes, bigger than China.

Freemium

Slang term. A common business model, particularly in selling **apps**, is to make the main product available for free but then to charge for certain features or additional content. It's a combination (or portmanteau if you're as pretentious as Tim) of "free" and "premium", in case you're wondering.

Glassdoor

http://www.glassdoor.co.uk

Best described as "TripAdvisor for companies", this international website allows employees and former employees to rate and review organisations they have worked for as employers. Anyone can start talking about a business – so if you employ people, someone else might just open your account for you.

Google+/G+

https://plus.google.com

Google+ is Google's attempt at a social network to compete with Facebook. It hasn't been anywhere near as successful in terms of sheer numbers as Facebook but it does have some very cool features that we love – such as Google Hangouts which is a better version of Skype. It's underrated, arguably underused and there is regularly discussion about whether or not Google will "kill it off".

Hashtag/#

Popularised by Twitter – to the extent that Facebook had to recognise them too – the hashtag is basically a keyword that allows you to tag or "file" a tweet against a particular subject so that if you search for that particular term, you get a list of tweets which contain it, regardless of whether or not you follow those people. So you can immediately see how using hashtags properly can extend the reach of your tweets as they won't necessarily just be seen by your followers.

Who comes up with hashtags? Well, anyone. You can start a hashtag if you want to – just stick the hash (or pound sign if you're American) in front of some text. There are some common ongoing hashtags such as #FF which stands for "Follow Friday" in which Twitter users suggest other users that people should follow. The trick is finding out which ones apply to you and/or your business. Working in HR, we use #HR and #hrblogs quite a lot. Sometimes events have their own hashtags so you know that tweets that contain them are from or inspired by that event.

The hashtag has become such a common part of the language on Twitter that regular users often use a hashtag in a jokey way, usually to finish off a tweet, such as "Just ended up in McDonalds for lunch #dietfail".

Instagram

https://instagram.com

Instagram is a social media site with photographs (and a bit of video), rather than status updates, at its heart. It is very straightforward as social media sites go (upload photo, say a little bit about it) but one of its most appealing factors is the ability to apply "filters" to your photos which can make them look pretty cool, if we do say so ourselves. It is entirely acceptable to post photos of your breakfast/lunch/dinner on Instagram and anyone who tells you otherwise is lying.

Internet of Things

This is one of those terms that has such massive reach and coverage that it could easily fill a book on its own. Basically it is a general term used to describe the current move towards all sorts of devices being connected and operated through or via the internet. The possibilities are endless and we are only just beginning to get our heads around them. Imagine your fridge knew what you'd just taken out of it and could add it automatically to your next online shopping order. That's something the internet of things would take care of. A heart monitor that keeps an eye on your dicky ticker and can identify - before you even feel it - that something untoward is happening and can notify both you and your local Accident & Emergency? The internet of things makes these kinds of things possible. The potential applications are mind blowing.

IRL/In Real Life

Slang term, most often found on Twitter, to describe meeting someone physically (i.e. In Real Life) rather than communicating online, as in "It was fab to meet @HR_Gem IRL today".

Klout

https://klout.com

Klout is primarily a tool that enables you to measure your impact on social media. It uses information gathered from your social media profiles (such as how many people have read your status, interacted with you or shared your content) to generate a score which enables you to see how you are "performing". We're a bit suspicious of it to be honest as it feels a bit too forced. But it's pretty much the only universal standard metric out there at the moment.

LinkedIn

https://www.linkedin.com

Simply put, LinkedIn is "Facebook for professionals". It allows you to show off your career achievements and showcase yourself for the purpose of professional networking and/or seeking job opportunities. As we've said elsewhere in this book, we're not huge fans but we do feel we kind of have to have profiles and engage with it sometimes…

Pinterest

https://www.pinterest.com

An online virtual noticeboard: a place for "pinning" images, videos and links onto your own noticeboards, which can be public or private. You will find everything on there from recipes, wedding ideas, fitness inspiration and motivational quotes.

Search Engine Optimisation (SEO)

Something of a dark art of the modern world, SEO is designing and coding websites in such a way that they appear higher up the list of results when internet users search for certain key words – and therefore ultimately drive more traffic to the site.

Slack

https://slack.com

Slack describes itself as "A messaging app for teams". We think of it as part old skool internet message-board, part social media app. It has a number of advantages over the traditional email "Reply All" project management approach and it isn't public in that you have to join a particular "team" to see all their content. Slack operates on a **freemium** basis so you can give it a try for nothing and if your organisation is small will probably be able to continue using it for nowt. We even know people who use Slack to organise their social lives and keep in touch with friends.

SlideShare

www.slideshare.net

A site that allows presenters to share slide decks with their audience and indeed anyone on the internet. A simple way to maximise your production of content if you have to give a presentation at any stage! Why not upload your slides to SlideShare, write a quick blog that covers roughly what you said and then share it on your favourite social platforms?

Snail mail

Slang term used to describe traditional postal services as opposed to almost-instantaneous electronic mail (as no-one calls email any more).

Snapchat

https://snapchat.com

A messaging app. Users can take pictures or videos and add text or drawings to them, then share them with their friends. The user decides how long the 'snaps' are available for – but it's usually just a few seconds. Clearly this limits its business application a little, but there are still brands out there making the most of it. It has quite a young user demographic – the **selfie** is a very popular on SnapChat.

Trending

A term used mostly in connection with Twitter. It refers to hashtags, terms or words that are the most popular at any given time. Trends can be shown as worldwide or local. To make a conference or product hashtag trend is the Holy Grail of all social media coverage activity.

Tumblr

https://www.tumblr.com

Pronounced "Tumbler" (in case you were wondering), this site is arguably the simplest way to host your own blog as it does all of the hard work for you. You can upload text, images, video or quotes to your Tumblr blog and then share the link widely across other social networks. Ideal if you don't want to invest the time and energy into setting up a WordPress site or want to dip a toe into blogging.

Tweeps

Slang term used to describe followers on Twitter – it comes from Twitter people/Twitter peeps/Tweeps. One of Gem's favourite words.

TweetDeck

https://tweetdeck.twitter.com

A good example of an app/website that helps you use Twitter in a more flexible way than Twitter's own app. For example, you can have a number of different panels open at once showing your timeline, notifications, any tweets featuring a particular hashtag etc. You can also use TweetDeck to schedule tweets so that they tweet at a particular time on a particular day. Which is very handy if you're going to be away at a key moment.

Twitter

https://twitter.com

In case you hadn't noticed through the rest of this book, Twitter is officially our favourite social networking site. Officially known as a "micro-blogging" site, users have 140 characters in which to make posts. Posts can include images and video (usually as links) or just be links to content elsewhere. You can find people discussing almost anything on Twitter at any time so whatever you're into, professional or personal, you'll find it going on somewhere on here too. Without Twitter it's possible, indeed probable that we'd never have met and that would be a Very Bad Thing indeed.

Vlog

Not a Klingon word from Star Trek, honestly: a vlog is simply a blog using the medium of video rather than text. With the increasing availability of reasonable quality video recording – most smartphones now can achieve a suitable picture for uploading – some people choose to present their blog personally and upload it to YouTube. On the other hand, some people hear the sound of their own voice and scuttle immediately back to their keyboards.

Wearable technology

Fairly self-explanatory this one: if carrying a phone is too much effort for you, look forward to the much-hyped adoption of wearable tech. Google may have killed off Glass (the ones that looked like a pair of glasses) but the concept looks like it's here to stay as people get excited about their Apple watches. For now, they still need to be connected to smartphones but who knows how long that will last? Still regarded by many as the Next Big Thing.

WordPress

https://wordpress.com

This site allows you to build your own website or blog from scratch with a bare minimum of programming knowledge. If you want the flexibility of having your own website but don't want to spend years learning how to code, go here. The results can be very impressive and the possibilities are pretty much endless.

Yammer

https://www.yammer.com

Probably the biggest private internal social media platform (or **ESN**) used by employers to facilitate and encourage sharing and collaboration across organisations. It plays nicely with the Microsoft Office packages we all know and sort-of love and in the right hands can transform how organisations work together.

YouTube

www.youtube.com

Fundamentally a video-sharing website, it has become one of the most visited search engines in the world, which goes to show how much we love our video. You can find everything that could possibly be filmed on here from inspirational speeches and talks (check out TED talks) to a guy in his garage explaining how to change your car's headlight bulb, clips of your favourite TV programmes, fan tributes to movies and lots of pets doing funny things.

And Finally: Get Started on Twitter & LinkedIn

As we said at the start of this book, we recognise that for some people, social media is still a great unknown. We recognise that some people who buy this book won't have any presence on social at all yet. So if this applies to you, then here is a very brief handy guide on how to set up accounts on Twitter and LinkedIn just to get you started, and a summary of the specific language used on each site.

For the rest of you who are already out there, feel free to get on with tweeting and sharing.

Twitter

Go to www.twitter.com and follow the sign up process. It is a fairly straightforward process and Twitter will guide you through it.

As you go through signing up, Twitter will suggest a username for you (this is called your Twitter handle). For example, "@TimScottHR".

You don't have to follow their suggestion, but do choose something simple and memorable, and ideally that links to your business. Some popular names will be taken, so you might have to get inventive! Make sure it is something you can live with for the long term, otherwise you might find yourself changing it on your marketing material. Try not to make your username too long, as it may use up characters when you are tweeting or people are tweeting you.

When you have set up your account, the next step is to find some people to follow. Twitter will give you some suggestions to begin with, but try searching for people that you know who are already tweeting, or even a few celebrities just to get you started. The more people you follow, the more accurate Twitter's recommendations for new people to follow will become.

Set up a 'bio'. This is clearly stating who you are, and gives people an idea about what you will tweet about so they can decide if they want to follow you or not. It's generally ok on Twitter to put in a little something personal too, within reason. Check out our bios for some ideas! You can also include a link here to your website, which will help generate traffic for you in that direction.

Other stuff…

- You might find it useful to download the Twitter app for your phone, so you can tweet or check your time line on the go.

- Keep your eye on the 'notifications' tab at the top of the app or the desktop. This is where it will show if someone tweets with your Twitter handle. It is good practice to reply to them or engage back, even it is just a simple tweet to say… *'Hey @TimScottHR, thanks for sharing my blog post!'*

- If you follow someone, and decide you don't enjoy their tweets, you can just unfollow them at any time. Just go into their profile and click 'unfollow'.

- You can amend your bio or profile at any time, along with your privacy settings, by just going into the settings menu (it looks like a cog wheel on the top right hand side of the page).

- If you see a tweet you like, you can 'favourite' it – and it will stay in your favourites list so you can return to it.

- Twitter allows you to make your tweets private so only people who follow you directly can see them - but this really isn't any good for a business account.

- Follow people from your industry and competitors. It will help you understand what others are tweeting about.

Once you are set up – all you need to do is send your first tweet – and we have given you plenty of rules on that already!

LinkedIn

Go to www.linkedin.co.uk and follow the sign up process. You can do it via the app, but you might find it a little easier on a desktop – the user experience is a generally better there. LinkedIn will guide you through the set up process, so simply follow the steps, which is essentially all about setting up a personal profile to begin with.

This is all about you – your career history, your education and your skills. You can choose whether you make your profile publically available or just to your connections. You can amend this at any time in the 'settings' tab.

You can also add a description about you and your skills and experience (the summary), links to your website, a list of your skills, education and qualifications and join relevant groups.

Other stuff…

- LinkedIn will recommend to you people that you might know based on the information you input into your profile. You will see this on the right hand side of the page.

- Most companies have LinkedIn groups or pages. You can follow these for their updates.

- LinkedIn will highlight news and articles that might be of interest to you. These will appear at the top of the page.

- You can choose how much of your profile you make public, or just how much you show to the people you are connected with. Adjust this in your privacy settings.

- If you want to share content on LinkedIn, such as an article or blog post, you will find most online content has a 'share' button, or LinkedIn icon. Simply click, and up will pop a box for you to edit (you don't have to, but you can include a comment about it if you want) and then simply click the button to share the link with your network. Anything you share can be seen by any of your connections.

- As well as connecting with people on LinkedIn, you can follow people too. For example, you can follow business leaders or writers.

- You can also give recommendations to other people that you know or ask them to recommend you too.

Once your account is set up and your profile is complete, you can begin to connect with people. Start by searching for people that you already know. If you click onto their profile, you will see a button that allows you to send a connection request. On the desktop version, LinkedIn will ask you how you know the person. On the app, it just sends it. It is considered polite to personalise the request. For example, *"Hi Gem, we met at a networking event recently, it would be great to connect with you on LinkedIn"* is just fine.

There is one simple rule with LinkedIn. The more connections you have, the greater the reach of your profile and your brand messages. So get connecting!

Other people will begin to connect with you too. You can see these, along with messages and updates from your network, in the top right hand corner (on the desktop version). You can choose whether to accept or ignore those connection requests.

There is just one more thing to note about LinkedIn. You will get lots of notifications and emails from them unless you organise this. For example, if you join a group, you will automatically get a daily email telling you about activity in that group. This might very quickly become annoying. You can however manage this in your settings area. You can set your notifications to suit your needs.

We now have just one final thing to say….

Good luck and enjoy!

Gemma and Tim

www.ingramcontent.com/pod-product-compliance
Lightning Source LLC
Chambersburg PA
CBHW070106210526
45170CB00013B/767